BWI 9-22-11

Rising Stars

JADEN SMITH

By Kristen Rajczak

Gareth Stevens
Publishing

Please visit our website, www.garethstevens.com. For a free color catalog of all our high-quality books, call toll free 1-800-542-2595 or fax 1-877-542-2596.

Rajczak, Kristen.
 Jaden Smith / Kristen Rajczak.
     p. cm. — (Rising stars)
 Includes index.
 ISBN 978-1-4339-5892-2 (pbk.)
 ISBN 978-1-4339-5893-9 (6-pack)
 ISBN 978-1-4339-5890-8 (library binding)
 1. Smith, Jaden, 1998—Juvenile literature. 2. Actors—United States—Biography—Juvenile literature. I. Title.
 PN2287.S6125R35 2011
 791.4302'8092—dc22
 [B]

                          2010046422

First Edition

Published in 2012 by
Gareth Stevens Publishing
111 East 14th Street, Suite 349
New York, NY 10003

Designer: Katelyn E. Reynolds
Editor: Kristen Rajczak

Photo credits: Cover, pp. 1–32 (background) Shutterstock.com; cover, pp. 1, 25 Ethan Miller/Getty Images; p. 5 Gareth Cattermole/Getty Images; p. 7 Peter Kramer/Getty Images; p. 9 Kevin Winter/Getty Images; p. 11 Scott Gries/Getty Images; p. 13 Claire Greenway/Getty Images; p. 15 Frazer Harrison/Getty Images; p. 17 Jeffrey Mayer/WireImage; p. 19 Eric Charbonneau/Le Studio/WireImage; p. 21 Jason Merritt/Getty Images; p. 23 Toni Passig/Getty Images; p. 27 Jeff Kravitz/AMA2010/FilmMagic; p. 29 Pascal Le Segretain/Getty Images.

Printed in the United States of America

CPSIA compliance information: Batch #CS11GS: For further information contact Gareth Stevens, New York, New York at 1-800-542-2595.

Contents

Meet Jaden

Jaden Smith is a talented actor. He comes from a famous family.

Born and Raised

Jaden Christopher Syre Smith was born on July 8, 1998. His father is actor Will Smith. His mother is actor Jada Pinkett Smith. The Smith family lives in California.

Will Smith

Jaden has a younger sister named Willow. She acts and sings. Jaden also has an older half-brother named Trey.

Trey Smith

Jada Pinkett Smith

Willow Smith

TV Tot

Jaden started acting when he was just 5 years old! He was on a TV show called *All of Us* for 2 years.

Working with Dad

Jaden's first movie came out in 2006. He and his dad, Will, played father and son. The movie was called *The Pursuit of Happyness*.

In 2007, Jaden received an MTV Movie Award and a Teen Choice Award for his part in *The Pursuit of Happyness*. He decided to keep acting.

15

Making Appearances

In 2008, Jaden was in an episode of the TV show *The Suite Life of Zack and Cody*. He was also in the music video for the Alicia Keys song "Superwoman."

More Movies

Jaden's next movie came out in 2008. *The Day the Earth Stood Still* also starred Keanu Reeves and Jennifer Connelly. Jaden played Jacob Benson.

Keanu Reeves

Jennifer Connelly

19

In 2010, Jaden made his biggest movie yet. He starred in *The Karate Kid*. The movie earned more than $175 million in the United States!

jaden
SMITH

Jackie Chan

21

Jaden trained for *The Karate Kid* for several months. He had to learn kung fu. He also went to China!

23

The Karate Kid made Jaden a superstar! He won an award for his work in the movie.

Branching Out

Jaden didn't just star in *The Karate Kid*. He rapped on Justin Bieber's song "Never Say Never." The song was on the movie soundtrack.

Justin Bieber

Jaden Smith is just starting a promising acting career. What's next for this young star?

Timeline

1998   Jaden Smith is born on July 8.

2003   Jaden starts acting in *All of Us*.

2006   Jaden stars in *The Pursuit of Happyness*.

2007   Jaden wins Teen Choice and MTV Movie Awards.

2008   Jaden is in *The Day the Earth Stood Still*.

2010   Jaden stars in *The Karate Kid*.

Books

Mattern, Joanne. *Jaden Smith*. Hockessin, DE: Mitchell Lane Publishers, 2010.

Tieck, Sarah. *Jaden Smith: Talented Actor*. Edina, MN: ABDO Publishing Company, 2011.

Websites

Jaden Smith

www.imdb.com/name/nm1535523/

Read more about the TV shows and movies Jaden has done.

The Karate Kid

www.karatekid-themovie.com/site/

Play games and see pictures and clips from the movie.

Glossary

award: a prize given for doing something well

career: a job someone has for a long time

episode: one part of a TV show's story

kung fu: a Chinese fighting sport

soundtrack: the songs used in a movie

talented: gifted

Index